PUBLIUS VIRGILIUS MARO

THE ECLOGUES

Translated into English verse by C. S. CALVERLEY

With an Introduction by MOSES HADAS

and Drawings by VERTÈS

NEW YORK

THE HERITAGE PRESS

VIRGIL'S ECLOGUES

Illustrated by Vertès

CONTENTS

INTRODUCTION

INTRODUCTION

1

Of all the stylish poetic forms whose vogue has passed, none is so alien to modern taste as the pastoral eclogue. It is not merely that exaggerated artifice, as in the case of women's fashions, is quickly demoded, or that mere passage of time makes a form obsolete, for Homer and tragedy and even the odes of Pindar, which are remoter in time and much more elaborate in artifice, are still read as poems, not merely as antiquarian curiosities. Artifice tends to be intrusive in the pastoral eclogue, as it is not in the earlier forms, because of a disharmony—not in proportions but in tone—between the artistic means and their ends.

The disharmony is there, probably, because the pastoral eclogue is an invention, not a gradual development out of what had gone before. The stages by which epic or tragedy reached maturity can be traced or plausibly surmised step by step; the eclogue seems to have been suddenly devised out of whole cloth by Theocritus in the first half of the third century B.C. But in actuality no literary form springs into being full-grown, like Athena from the head of Zeus. Theocritus, like his successors in pastoral, was a self-conscious litterateur, steeped in literary tradition. A glance at his antecedents which may have provided seed for Theocritus' work may illuminate the strength as well as the weakness of his innovation.

Among the older genres which may have affected Theocritean pastoral, three present aspects which appear to have determined its character; these are the mime, the utopian romance, and the hymn. The most obvious source is the mime because, like Theocritus' idylls, it employs fictive characters, dialogue, and usually a Sicilian setting. The term "mime" is a catchall for a variety of productions. In a broad sense the Greeks designated as mimes all manner of solo entertainers—singers, dancers, jugglers, conjurers, panto-mimes—whether they exhibited their skill at the banquet or in the market place. Literature is concerned only with such performers as recited mono-logues in the character of some amusing type, with dramatic and entertaining fidelity to manner and language. It may well be that persons so represented are the first fictive characters in European literature, for the persons of epic and tragedy were "historical."

At a level which far transcends their origins and normal development the dialogues of Plato may be regarded as mimes, and Plato is said to have learned this part of his business from the Sicilian Epicharmus. Sicily, indeed, was always the proper climate of the mimes, and left its mark in the Doricisms of their language. The mimes of the Sicilian Sophron were classified as "of men" and "of women," and we have such titles as *The Peasant, The Tunny Fisher, The Needlewoman, The Sorceress, The Mother-in-Law.* A later division, appli-cable to Theocritus, is of "urban" and "rural" mimes.

In the Hellenistic age writers of mimes were serious artists and were referred to as "biologists," or students of life; an enlightened Ptolemy who wished to understand the character of the people he ruled was advised to listen to the biologists. The extant mimes of Herondas justify this designa-tion, and so, to an eminent degree, does Theocritus 15, "The Women at the Festival of Adonis." Other of Theocritus' idylls retain some of the true character of the mime, but in most the "biological" element has been replaced by the purely pastoral. The Theocritean pastoral is in fact a new genre; its persons are not characters, and the songs they exchange not dialogue. It is the essence of the pastoral that imagination be so far as possible independent of reality.

In the sense that the pastoral poet creates his own world his very artificiality is capable of high seriousness. By disdaining the world of the familiar, fashioning a secluded Arcadia according to his heart's desire and peopling it with a cast free from the constraints of ordinary convention, the pastoral poet may not only attain the highest reaches of imaginative creativity but also provide himself with something like a rigged experimental field for examining the nature of man's potentialities. For this, too, classical Greek literature provided paradigms. The realm of the Phæacians in the *Odyssey*, and a series of Old Comedy plays, of which Aristophanes' *Birds* is the best example, show how the rigged field may be used for studying man. The possibilities of the form may be illustrated by Longus' *Daphnis and Chloe*, which, though in prose and centuries later than Theocritus, is yet our fullest pastoral. Here the author frankly avows that he has composed an imaginary story—a pendant to a picture he had seen—to illustrate the workings of love. He rigs his field in a secluded valley, chooses as his subjects two foundlings whose maturation in love is to be studied, introduces a series of selected intruders from the outside world to observe their effects upon the process, and when the process is complete the experiment is concluded and the subjects assume a place in conventional society. Theocritus' idylls, it is true, only skirt the experimental possibilities of the pastoral, but Virgil's "Messianic Eclogue" does limn a serious utopia, and so do some of the humanist pastorals. Contemporary science fiction may prove to be a somewhat bizarre reincarnation of the pastoral in this sense.

The least obvious but perhaps most significant of the antecedents of the pastoral eclogue is the hymn. From the seventh and sixth centuries B.C. we have a group of poems called *Homeric Hymns*, though Homer was not their author. They were intended for liturgical use in connection with festivals of the major deities, and each celebrates its particular deity by recounting instances of his prowess in the field of his peculiar potency. It is hard for people nurtured in a puritanical religious tradition to conceive of an elaborate account of Aphrodite's seduction of Anchises or of Hermes' prodigious roguery as part of a religious service, but if love and agile wit are essential ingredients of a successful life it is appropriate that their patrons be glorified by celebrating their mastery in them.

The finest of the Hymns is *To Demeter*, which describes the seizure of Persephone by Hades, the grief of her mother Demeter which she assuages by caring for a mortal infant at Eleusis, her vengeance on gods and men by causing famine, the restoration of Persephone during the growing season of each year, and the establishment of the Eleusinian Mysteries to commemorate her sorrows and her reconciliation. The profoundly religious atmosphere of the poem is palpable; indeed its fragrance and gentleness, its fusion of human warmth and divine majesty, approach our own notions of religion very nearly. And yet if the poem were printed in a collection of pastoral masques its religious quality would not be noticed. There is the familiar profusion of flowers, the pretty girls bearing rustic names, the masquerade of important personages as inferiors, the eventual unmasking and reconciliation. It is easy to understand how a poem like *To Demeter* would be cherished for its aesthetic values long after its religious meaning had faded.

The key to much Hellenistic art, including literature, is its apparent obliviousness of the original religious associations of the forms it cultivated for purely aesthetic reasons. Callimachus wrote hymns like the Homeric but with no genuine religious feeling, and the fact that his and the *Homeric Hymns* are combined in our manuscript tradition shows that the later Greeks sensed no real distinction between the two. The historical sense which enables us to adjust our sights to earlier modes of thought and expression is a modern development; the Alexandrians assumed that their own standards had always applied. If their motivation was art for art's sake they could not conceive that the motivation of the classics was different. Apollonius of Rhodes doubtless thought that in his *Argonautica* he was doing with sophisticated technique and recondite materials what Homer had done naively and with obvious materials, without realizing the essential difference between his poem and Homer's.

It may well be that Theocritus similarly misconceived, or was indifferent to, the true nature of the *Homeric Hymns*, and specifically the hymn to Demeter, when he embarked on his idylls. One outward indication that this was so is his hexameter verse. The hexameter is the stateliest of Greek measures and exactly right for intoning a formal hymn; but Theocritus' idylls contain rustic songs, for which lyric meter and strophic arrangement, not recitative verses of identical pattern, are expected. A hexameter song is a contradiction in terms; Theocritus may have committed the anomaly because it was established in the tradition he thought he was following.

Aside from his use of the unsuitable meter for songs, it is the use of the hexameter to describe the doings of country bumpkins which affords us the clearest index to the strength and weakness of Theocritus, as of his followers. In classical usage the hexameter is firmly associated with the deeds of genuine gods and genuine heroes. When Solon or Theognis came to speak out on contemporary political and social questions in their own persons, the less stately elegiac meter came into use; and when a more subjective and anti-heroic mood arose, the vulgar iambic was its mode of expression. The regular meter of the mime, in Herondas for example but not in Theocritus, is iambic. The direction of Greek literature as a whole is from the heroic to the bourgeois; Euripides, New Comedy, the prose romance, are successive landmarks in the process. Callimachus and Apollonius do use the hexameter, but as conscious archaizers. The story of the *Argonautica* takes place in the heroic age and heroic personages figure in it; but Jason is in effect an Alexandrian dandy, and Athena and Hera are fashionable Alexandrian matrons. Only in the fifth century A.D. do we find an attempt to dignify an essentially bourgeois story, in Musæus' *Hero and Leander*, by putting it into the heroic meter and concluding it with the tragic death which is the hero's hallmark.

We can see the magnitude of Theocritus' innovation in frankly making bumpkins his theme, and some eight centuries before Musæus, and we can also see the source of his equivocations. Sometimes, as in the "Harvest Home" (Idyll 7), the rustic exteriors are masquerades for gentlemen-poets; sometimes there is a patronizing air of slumming; sometimes the ambiguities are unresolved. The remarkable thing is that, despite the artificialities inherent in his innovation and inseparable from his age, Theocritus is a true poet of man and nature. He has a sympathy for ordinary humanity based upon accurate psychological understanding, and if this is not altogether new his equally sympathetic perception of the sights and sounds of the countryside is.

It may be that this new attention to nature is a result of Cynic teachings; it may be that it is a sort of escapism from the refined elegance of the Alexandrian court, such as would appeal to the denizen of any great metropolis today. It is true, especially in the "Harvest Home," that the rusticity has the spuriousness of a Marie Antoinette pretending to be a milkmaid, and yet the relaxed delight of a full-blown late-summer day is nowhere better communicated. If Theocritus is not a man to rise before dawn for chores in the barn when he could have room service, he has clearly seen and heard and smelled fields and animals and has not been repelled. The fault of the long succession of epigoni whose denatured and beribboned rusticity has cloyed our taste for pastoral poetry is that neither they nor their mouthpieces have ever got nearer to nature than the books of their predecessors. Plucked shepherds with lace cuffs have nothing of interest to say to anyone except powdered shepherdesses in hoops.

And yet the trivial shells to which poetic forms are reduced when they have been emptied of their serious meaning often acquire a new burden of seriousness. So it was with classical epic and tragedy, and so it was with pastoral also. The serious possibilities adumbrated in Theocritus, as indicated above, were realized in such poems as Bion's *Lament for Adonis*, Virgil's "Messianic Eclogue," Spenser's *Shephearde's Calendar*, Milton's *Lycidas*. Virgil's *Eclogues*, which are our special concern, traverse the whole range of pastoral, from empty prettiness to sketching the outlines of a brave new world.

2

A survey of the Greek antecedents of pastoral can be as useful for an appreciation of Virgil's work as of Theocritus', for the elements which formed Theocritus were by his poetry channeled into Virgil's. Latin poetry in all genres was wholly subject to Greek canons, so that Roman poets could base their claim to originality on having been the first to introduce a given Greek form into Latin. The Greek literature that was most familiar to Romans was the Alexandrian, which was nearest in time and temper; but some discriminating writers, like Horace, turned to the classical period to find models for their best work. Virgil too moved backward in time as his art progressed. For the *Æneid*, which is his last and greatest work, he emulated Homer himself, with erotic or sensational matter, like the Dido episode, borrowed from the Alexandrian Apollonius. The *Eclogues*, which are his earliest work, aside from the doubtful juvenilia of the *Virgilian Appendix*, are an avowed imitation of Theocritus.

Several of Virgil's *Eclogues* were evoked by a particular event in his career, and their publication materially affected the subsequent directions of his work; it is therefore worth our while to glance at the outlines of the poet's life. Virgil was born 15 October, 70 B.C., at Andes, a small village near Mantua, in what was then Cisalpine Gaul. His father was a prosperous farmer, and Virgil was sent to school to Cremona and Milan, and later to Naples and Rome, where he studied Greek literature, rhetoric, and Epicurean philosophy. His rural beginnings explain the deep and knowledgeable attachment to the countryside and its occupations which is reflected in the *Eclogues* and which forms the substance of the *Georgics*. His early sympathy for Epicureanism is indicated by a number of passages in his works; a line like *Felix qui potuit rerum cognoscere causas*, "Blessed the man who availed to discern the causes of things" (*Georgics* 2.489), is a plain allusion to Lucretius, who was the Roman herald of Epicureanism. But Epicureanism was officially frowned upon in the incipient empire because it denied divine concern for human affairs and hence questioned the religious sanction which was the justification for authoritarian government.

And yet the *Æneid*, which is Virgil's maturest and profoundest work, might be described quite accurately as a solemn justification of Augustus' authoritarianism on the basis of a religious sanction. The youthful radical who matures into a supporter of existing institutions is a common enough phenomenon, and the sincerity of a conversion to the Augustan principate cannot be questioned; to this day no political theorist has been able to point to a feasible alternative for bringing the political chaos and bloody civil wars of Rome to an end. Nevertheless the fact remains that Virgil's career as apologist for the principate began with special privileges bestowed upon him by the youthful but shrewd Octavian who became Augustus.

The circumstances were as follows: When Brutus and Cassius were defeated at Philippi in 42 B.C., all power passed into the hands of Octavian and his fellow triumvirs Antony and Lepidus. They had promised their soldiers farms as bonuses, and among the lands to be expropriated for the purpose was the farm of Virgil's father. Virgil's early poetizing, perhaps some of the eclogues in our collection, had engaged the interest of Asinius Pollio, who was governor of Cisalpine Gaul and himself a scholar and poet. Pollio procured Virgil an audience with Octavian, in consequence of which his farm was restored to him and he became a protégé of Mæcenas, who was in effect Octavian's minister of public relations.

It was at Mæcenas' request that Virgil composed the four books of the *Georgics*, whose object was to proclaim the special blessedness of Italy and to promote a return to agriculture and the traditional ways of Rome. And it was at Mæcenas' suggestion that he wrote the *Æneid*, whose object was to show that Rome was divinely ordained to rule the world and Augustus divinely appointed to direct Rome's destiny. It was Virgil who introduced Horace to Mæcenas; Horace, who mentions Virgil with affection in several passages, became an important member of the circle of Mæcenas and virtual poet laureate.

Virgil fell into his last illness on a journey home from Greece in company with Augustus, and died at Brundisium 22 September, 19 B.C.

3

It is in the *Eclogues* that we see the young country poet transformed into a familiar of the imperial circle, the avowed imitator into an artist who has found his own voice. The collection contains ten pieces, which appear to have been written between 42 and 39 B.C., when Virgil was about thirty. Their probable chronological order is determined in part by their degree of independence of Theocritean models and in part by their dedications. Eclogues 2, 3, 5, and 7 are purely imitative and were surely the first written, probably in the order of their numbering. Eclogues 4 and 8 are addressed to Pollio; references to Pollio's consulship and to his victory over the Parthini show that they were written in 40 and 39 B.C., respectively. Eclogues 6 and 9, which concern the recovery of Virgil's farm, are addressed to Alfenus Varus, who was Pollio's successor as governor of Cisalpine Gaul. The first word in Eclogue 10, addressed to Virgil's friend Gallus, declares that it is last in order, but that position surely belongs to Eclogue 1, which is addressed to the emperor and serves to dedicate the entire collection to him.

We proceed now to brief summaries and comments on the individual poems, following the traditional numbering.

Eclogue 1 is in the form of a dialogue between two shepherds: Melibœus, who has been driven from his farm and is dejectedly driving his woebegone herd with no known destination, and Tityrus, representing Virgil, who is reposing at ease among his contented sheep in his own field and singing of his Amaryllis. To Melibœus' questions, prompted by curiosity rather than envy, Tityrus replies that he had gone to the wonderful city of Rome to obtain freedom and had there been told by a marvellous youth, "Feed still your kine." His benefactor he would always regard as a veritable god and would offer sacrifice to him regularly. The change in his fortunes had come when he released himself from bondage to Galatea and transferred his affections to Amaryllis. Melibœus laments the loss, to some barbarian, of the familiar homestead upon which he had so long labored, and his own exile to some alien land; and Tityrus offers him hospitality for the evening.

What we have here, to all appearances, is an expression of gratitude on the part of the poet, somewhat excessive, perhaps, but not out of keeping with the form, which is a perfectly traditional pastoral. There is the thoroughly bucolic background; there are the rustic speakers with their rustic concerns and behavior, especially their awe at the wonders of the big city; and there is the masquerade. Tityrus is identified as Virgil not by any particular psychological traits but merely by the fact that a confiscated farm has been restored to him. It is entirely possible that Melibœus too represents a real person. He has been very badly used, and the fact that he does not recriminate the "god" whose caprice has benefited his interlocutor makes the injustice more poignant. Forsaken Galatea and her supplanter Amaryllis may only be the country wenches who are the regular appurtenance of versified shepherds; but forsaking the one and embracing the other have brought Tityrus his prosperity—which the misery of decent Melibœus makes seem a little tainted. Perhaps it was not merely from one wench to another that Virgil transferred his love. If that is what was in Virgil's mind, then there is bitterness in his self-abasement before his new-found god. When he vows that his loyalty will endure until beasts fly and fishes walk he is using a standard figure which the Greek rhetoricians called *adynata*, or impossibilities, but there may be significance in the notion of Parthians drinking of a Gaulish river and Gauls of a Parthian. The probability is that Virgil intended only what meets the eye; but we cannot dismiss the possibility that Eclogue 1 is a heartfelt denunciation of injustice and a bitter self-indictment for surrender of integrity. The vulgar agitator must rant; the poet need not be so obvious.

Eclogue 2, which is possibly the earliest in time, represents the shepherd Corydon as lamenting his failure to win the beautiful Alexis. The poem is clearly modeled upon Theocritus 11, in which the uncouth but pathetic Polyphemus laments his want of success with the sea-nymph Galatea. As in the Theocritean model so here the frustrated lover cites his self-neglecting devotion, calls attention to his wealth, protests that his reflection in the water shows him not to be really ugly; but in addition Corydon boasts of his ability to sing. If Alexis will relent, Corydon will share his music with him, though a girl named Thestylis is eager for his love. Pallas does indeed favor townsmen, but rustics have their tutelary deities also. If our eclogue is nothing more than an imitation it must be confessed that it is far inferior to its model. Virgil has nothing like the childish monster, the inhuman fair, the enchanting setting in the sea; and the substitution of a pretty boy for the sea-nymph further debases the original. But there is reason to think that Corydon may represent Virgil himself, and if Corydon is a masquerade then the other figures may be identifiable also. It may be then that here too the conventions of the pastoral conceal an intensely felt drama.

Eclogue 3, which is largely adapted from Theocritus 4 and 5, is also probably an early piece. For the first sixty lines the shepherds Menalcas and Damon abuse each other, and then decide to engage in a poetic contest, with a cow and two fine cups as a wager and Palæmon as judge. In the next forty-odd lines the contestants alternate their "amœbæan" or "interchange" verses, and the poem concludes with the umpire declaring that he cannot choose between them. Contests of this kind seem to have been a popular pastime, and there is no need to search for hidden identifications and significances, though such may be present.

Eclogue 4, called the "Pollio," or more usually the "Messianic Eclogue," is far the best known of all. Its prophecy of the advent of a "newborn babe— who first shall end/That age of iron, bid a golden dawn/Upon the broad world" was understood, from the time of Constantine and Eusebius until the nineteenth century, to refer to the Christ; and it was the belief that Virgil did indeed foretell the birth of Christ that gave him almost the prestige of a saint in western Christendom. Alexander Pope imitated this eclogue in his *Messiah*, which he called "A sacred Eclogue in imitation of Virgil's Pollio." Modern scholars have ransacked every corner of the eastern Mediterranean to find the sources for Virgil's apocalyptic ideas and expressions. Actually we need go no farther than Isaiah for the ultimate source. Mention of the Sybil in line 3 points to the (extant) *Sibylline Oracles*, of which Books 3-5 are surely of Jewish or Christian origin. Eclogue 4, in turn, with its picture of history as divinely planned and controlled with its administration entrusted to Rome and Rome's ruler, is in effect a blueprint for the *Æneid*.

What child it was whose birth was to usher in the new world order is uncertain. The easiest surmise is that it was a child Pollio was expecting, but it may have been Octavian's—which turned out to be a girl, and eventually a very naughty girl. Except for its flowers and fruits and peaceful domestic animals and its deprecation of voyaging and commerce there is not much of the conventional pastoral in this "loftier song," but in its relegation of the familiar world and vision of a new and better order it reaches the extreme of the pastoral's potential.

Eclogue 5 is an amœbæan poem in which two shepherds, Mopsus and Menalcas, engage in a contest of song. After twenty lines of introductory exchanges Mopsus sings of the death of Daphnis, and Menalcas of his deification. Daphnis is the ideal shepherd of pastoral, and his death is sung by Thyrsis in the first idyll of Theocritus; so far Eclogue 5 is merely another imitation of a Theocritean model. But there is a strong probability that Daphnis stands for Julius Cæsar, in which case it is Cæsar's death and transfiguration that are here represented. Again the artful conventions of the pastoral may be a vehicle for serious content and not merely an ingenious pastime.

Eclogue 6 is addressed to Varus, who superseded Pollio as governor of Cisalpine Gaul and who helped Virgil assert his rights to his farm against a centurion who is said to have abused Virgil physically. The eclogue starts with an apology to Varus for not singing his epic achievements: Apollo had warned the poet to confine himself to pastoral. The body of the eclogue tells how two shepherds found Silenus asleep after a debauch, tied him with his own garlands, and exacted a song from him. The fauns and the beasts danced to his music and the oaks swayed their heads. The first part of his song described creation, the juncture of atoms in the void to form the universe, and the emergence of order out of chaos as sea and land and sun and clouds and verdure and living animals took shape. The concluding part recounted the stories of a series of mythological personages which possessed symbolic meaning. The cosmogonic portion, which is clearly influenced by Lucretius, and the mythologic, which has certain Hellenistic affinities, constitute a serious approach to a first philosophy. Aside from the poetic conventions observed, there is genuine poetry in the expression of a true sense of wonder. The fact that the pastoral form is here so clearly ancillary to a deeper content suggests that it may be so also in poems where it is less clearly ancillary.

Eclogue 7 is Melibœus' account of an amœbæan contest between the shepherd Thyrsis and the goatherd Corydon. The poem is a conventional pastoral, with motifs imitated from several of Theocritus' idylls. It justifies itself completely as pure pastoral; whether some masquerade or symbolic meaning is involved is hard to divine.

Eclogue 8 is addressed to Pollio on the occasion of his return from a victory over the Parthini in Illyria. It is an amœbæan poem, in which Damon first describes his grief for the faithlessness of his beloved Nisa, and then Alphesibœus the efforts of an unnamed lady to bring her laggard lover Daphnis back to her by means of magic. Damon's lines on his first encounter with his sweetheart are perhaps the most appealing in all the *Eclogues:*

> *Within our orchard-walls I saw thee first,*
> *A wee child with her mother—(I was sent*
> *To guide you)—gathering apples wet with dew.*
> *Ten years and one I scarce had numbered then;*
> *Could scarce on tiptoe reach the brittle boughs.*
> *I saw, I fell, I was myself no more.*

The story in Alphesibœus' part is copied from Theocritus' deeply moving

Idyll 2. There the forlorn girl, who despairs of the efficacy of her magic but must use every means to save herself, and her careless gallant are characterized with economy and exquisite perception. By Virgil's time the situation had become a literary cliché, and Virgil's reworking of it seems little more than a skillful exercise.

Eclogue 9 is the fullest, and possibly the earliest, treatment of the episode of the recovered farm, which is dealt with also in Eclogues 6 and 1. The story is told in a conversation between two shepherds, Lycidas and Mœris, who meet on a country road. Mœris has been turned out of his farm and is taking kids to market for the new owner. Lycidas had heard that the poetry of Menalcas (who represents Virgil) had saved the district, and Mœris informs him that he and Menalcas himself had barely escaped physical danger. The two go on their way recalling Menalcas' songs beginning:

> *Varus! thy name, if Mantua still be ours—*
> *(Mantua! to poor Cremona all too near)*

and

> *Daphnis! why watch those old-world planets rise?*
> *Lo! onward marches sacred Cæsar's star*

and singing snatches of others. The device of making a pair of literary shepherds discuss poets and poetry while walking in the country is borrowed from Theocritus' Idyll 7.

Eclogue 10 is addressed to Cornelius Gallus, some four years older than Virgil, and acknowledged to be one of the greatest poets of Rome. Gallus served Octavian in distributing lands in northern Italy, later fought at Actium, and received the enormously important post of first Roman governor of Egypt. There he committed some serious indiscretion, whose nature is unknown to us, and died by his own hand in 26 B.C. It is probably because of his disgrace that his poetry has not survived.

In the opening lines Virgil declares that this pastoral is to be his last; possibly he was already at work on the *Georgics*. The object of the poem is to console Gallus for the loss of his love Lycoris. Eclogue 10 is perhaps the most artificial of all, and at the same time the best example of how beautiful sheer artifice can be. Looked at baldly, what we have is a description of how a Roman officer on active service was jilted by a notorious actress, how he was informed of her faithlessness by rustic deities who sought to comfort him, how he imagined himself an Arcadian shepherd, reckless of discomfort, roaming with nymphs, and shooting the "Cretan arrow from the Parthian bow." Looked at less puritanically, what we have is common, even vulgar, experience transformed by art into a world so exquisitely wrought that the commonplace cannot impinge upon it.

4

Poetry is impossible to translate. A strong story moving in bright sunlight, like the *Iliad*, can be rendered tolerably well in another language; for however much may evaporate in the process, enough of the vital residue remains. Even a narrative that moves in half-lights and communicates much more than it says, like the *Æneid*, becomes much harder to render and appreciate in another language. The more the poet asserts himself over his story, in other words, the more difficult is translation; and therefore lyric, which is the most subjective of all, is the most difficult to render. Pindar or Horace must become grotesque or banal in translation, and the only feasible solution is for the translator, who must himself be a poet, to write another poem which may produce a similar effect. But then the merit of the poem is in direct ratio to the liberty it takes with its original.

Translating highly stylized pastoral imposes special difficulties. Here there is least room for independence, since the artificialities, which are of the essence, must be retained. What is wanted is not originality but high technical proficiency in meter and language, mastery of a special vocabulary including archaic and dialectical forms, and a talent for imitation. The translator must have the gift of the good parodist without his comic intention. For a poet of the first rank this amounts to self-effacement, and that is why we have so few satisfactory translations of ancient pastoral.

Of those we have, the best are the work of Charles Stuart Calverley (1831-1884). Calverley wrote a great deal of light verse, which was enormously popular in its time; his major serious production is his translation of Theocritus, which is highly esteemed to this day. His version of the *Eclogues*, here presented, was made after the success of the Theocritus, and is less well known because the *Eclogues* occupy a lesser place in the history of literature. Calverley was a good scholar—he was Fellow of Christ's in Cambridge, where he had taken medals in Greek and Latin—and a good versifier; it is evidence of his recognition of his own gifts and his own limitations that it was the *Eclogues*, not the *Æneid* or the *Georgics*, that he chose to render. His gifts, as recorded in the entry under his name in the *Dictionary of National Biography*, included "unique powers of imitation" which made him "perhaps the best parodist in the language."

MOSES HADAS

THE ECLOGUES

OF VIRGIL

E C L O G U E

I

~~~~~~

MELIBŒUS   TITYRUS

MELIBŒUS

Stretched in the shadow of the broad beech, thou

Rehearsest, Tityrus, on the slender pipe

Thy woodland music. We our fatherland

Are leaving, we must shun the fields we love:

While, Tityrus, thou, at ease amid the shade,

Bidd'st answering woods call Amaryllis "fair."

TITYRUS

O Melibœus! 'Tis a god that made

For me this holiday: for god I'll aye

Account him; many a young lamb from my fold

Shall stain his altar. Thanks to him, my kine

Range, as thou seest them: thanks to him, I play

What songs I list upon my shepherd's pipe.

MELIBŒUS

For me, I grudge thee not; I marvel much:

So sore a trouble is in all the land.

Lo! feeble I am driving hence my goats—

Nay dragging, Tityrus, one, and that with pain.

For, yeaning here amidst the hazel-stems,

She left her twin kids—on the naked flint

She left them; and I lost my promised flock.

This evil, I remember, oftentimes,

4

(Had not my wits been wandering,) oaks foretold

By heaven's hand smitten: oft the wicked crow

Croaked the same message from the rifted holm.

—Yet tell me, Tityrus, of this 'God' of thine.

TITYRUS

The city men call Rome my folly deemed

Was e'en like this of ours, where week by week

We shepherds journey with our weanling flocks.

So whelp to dog, so kid (I knew) to dam

Was likest: and I judged great things by small.

But o'er all cities this so lifts her head,

As doth o'er osiers lithe the cypress tree.

MELIBŒUS

What made thee then so keen to look on Rome?

TITYRUS

Freedom: who marked, at last, my helpless state:

5

Now that a whiter beard than that of yore

Fell from my razor: still she marked, and came

(All late) to help me—now that all my thought

Is Amaryllis, Galatea gone.

While Galatea's, I despaired, I own,

Of freedom, and of thrift. Though from my farm

Full many a victim stept, though rich the cheese

Pressed for yon thankless city: still my hand

Returned not, heavy with brass pieces, home.

MELIBŒUS

I wondered, Amaryllis, whence that woe,

And those appeals to heav'n: for whom the peach

Hung undisturbed upon the parent tree

Tityrus was gone! Why, Tityrus, pine and rill,

And all these copses, cried to thee,"Come home!"

8

TITYRUS

What could I do? I could not step from out

My bonds; nor meet, save there, with Pow'rs so kind.

There, Melibœus, I beheld that youth

For whom each year twelve days my altars smoke.

Thus answered he my yet unanswered prayer;

"Feed still, my lads, your kine, and yoke your bulls."

MELIBŒUS

Happy old man! Thy lands are yet thine own!

Lands broad enough for thee, although bare stones

And marsh choke every field with reedy mud.

Strange pastures shall not vex thy teeming ewes,

Nor neighbouring flocks shed o'er them rank disease.

Happy old man! Here, by familiar streams

And holy springs, thou'lt catch the leafy cool.

Here, as of old, yon hedge, thy boundary line,

Its willow-buds a feast for Hybla's bees,

Shall with soft whisperings woo thee to thy sleep.

Here, 'neath the tall cliff, shall the vintager

Sing carols to the winds: while all the time

Thy pets, the stockdoves, and the turtles make

Incessantly their moan from aëry elms.

TITYRUS

Aye, and for this shall slim stags graze in air,

And ocean cast on shore the shrinking fish;

For this, each realm by either wandered o'er,

Parthians shall Arar drink, or Tigris Gauls;

Ere from this memory shall fade that face!

MELIBŒUS

And we the while must thirst on Libya's sands,

O'er Scythia roam, and where the Cretan stems

The swift Oaxes; or, with Britons, live

Shut out from all the world. Shall I e'er see,

In far-off years, my fatherland? the turf

That roofs my meagre hut? see, wondering last,

Those few scant cornblades that are realms to me?

What! must rude soldiers hold these fallows trim?

That corn barbarians? See what comes of strife,

Poor people—where we sowed, what hands shall reap!

Now, Melibœus, pr'ythee graft thy pears,

And range thy vines! Nay on, my she-goats, on,

Once happy flock! For never more must I,

Outstretched in some green hollow, watch you hang

From tufted crags, far up: no carols more

I'll sing: nor, shepherded by me, shall ye

Crop the tart willow and the clover-bloom.

TITYRUS

Yet here, this one night, thou may'st rest with me,

Thy bed green branches. Chestnuts soft have I

And mealy apples, and our fill of cheese.

Already, see, the far-off chimneys smoke,

And deeper grow the shadows of the hills.

E C L O G U E

II

~~~~~~

CORYDON

CORYDON

For one fair face—his master's idol—burned

The shepherd Corydon; and hope had none.

Day after day he came ('twas all he could)

Where, piles of shadow, thick the beeches rose:

There, all alone, his unwrought phrases flung,

Bootless as passionate, to copse and crag:

13

"Hardhearted! Naught car'st thou for all my songs,

Naught pitiest. I shall die, one day, for thee.

The very cattle court cool shadows now,

Now the green lizard hides beneath the thorn:

And for the reaper, faint with driving heat,

The handmaids mix the garlic-salad strong.

My only mates, the crickets—as I track

'Neath the fierce sun thy steps—make shrill the woods.

Better to endure the passion and the pride

Of Amaryllis: better to endure

Menalcas—dark albeit as thou art fair.

Put not, oh fair, in difference of hue

Faith overmuch: the white May-blossoms drop

And die; the hyacinth swart, men gather it.

Thy scorn am I: thou ask'st not whence I am,

How rich in snowy flocks, how stored with milk.

14

O'er Sicily's green hills a thousand lambs

Wander, all mine: my new milk fails me not

In summer or in snow. Then I can sing

All songs Amphion the Dircæan sang,

Piping his flocks from Attic Aracynth.

Nor am I all uncouth. For yesterday,

When winds had laid the seas, I, from the shore,

Beheld my image. Little need I fear

Daphnis, though thou wert judge, or mirrors lie.

—Oh! be content to haunt ungentle fields,

A cottager, with me; bring down the stag,

And with green switch drive home thy flocks of kids:

Like mine, thy woodland songs shall rival Pan's!

—'Twas Pan first taught us reed on reed to fit

With wax: Pan watches herd and herdsman too.

—Nor blush that reeds should chafe thy pretty lip.

16

What pains Amyntas took, this skill to gain!

I have a pipe—seven stalks of different lengths

Compose it—which Damœtas gave me once.

Dying he said, "At last 'tis all thine own."

The fool Amyntas heard, and grudged, the praise.

Two fawns moreover (perilous was the gorge

Down which I tracked them!)—dappled still each skin—

Drain daily two ewe-udders; all for thee.

Long Thestylis has cried to make them hers.

Hers be they—since to thee my gifts are dross.

"Be mine, oh fairest! See! for thee the Nymphs

Bear baskets lily-laden: Naiads bright

For thee crop poppy-crests and violets pale,

With daffodil and fragrant fennel-bloom:

Then, weaving cassia in and all sweet things,

Soft hyacinth paint with yellow marigold.

Apples I'll bring thee, hoar with tender bloom,

And chestnuts—which my Amaryllis loved,

And waxen plums: let plums too have their day.

And thee I'll pluck, oh bay, and, myrtle, thee

Its neighbour: neighboured thus your sweets shall mix.

—Pooh! Thou'rt a yokel, Corydon. Thy love

Laughs at thy gifts: if gifts must win the day,

Rich is Iolas. What thing have I,

Poor I, been asking—while the winds and boars

Ran riot in my pools and o'er my flowers?

"—Yet, fool, whom fliest thou? Gods have dwelt in woods,

And Dardan Paris. Citadels let her

Who built them, Pallas, haunt: green woods for me.

Grim lions hunt the wolf, and wolves the kid,

And kids at play the clover-bloom. I hunt

Thee only: each one drawn to what he loves.

See! trailing from their necks the kine bring home

The plough, and, as he sinks, the sun draws out

To twice their length the shadows. Still I burn

With love. For what can end or alter love?"

Thou'rt raving, simply raving, Corydon.

Clings to thy leafy elm thy half-pruned vine.

Why not begin, at least, to plait with twigs

And limber reeds some useful homely thing?

Thou'lt find another love, if scorned by this.

E C L O G U E

III

~~~~~~

MENALCAS   DAMŒTAS   PALÆMON

MENALCAS

Whose flock, Damœtas? Melibœus's?

DAMŒTAS

No, Ægon's. Ægon left it in my care.

MENALCAS

Unluckiest of flocks! Your master courts

Neæra, wondering if she like me more:

21

Meanwhile a stranger milks you twice an hour,

Saps the flock's strength, and robs the suckling lambs.

DAMŒTAS

Yet fling more charily such words at men.

You—while the goats looked goatish—we know who,

And in what chapel—(but the kind Nymphs laughed)—

MENALCAS

Then (was it?) when they saw me Micon's shrubs

And young vines hacking with my rascally knife?

DAMŒTAS

Or when by this old beech you broke the bow

And shafts of Daphnis: which you cried to see,

You crossgrained lad, first given to the boy;

And harm him somehow you must needs, or die.

MENALCAS

Where will lords stop, when knaves are come to this?

22

Did not I see you, scoundrel, in a snare

Take Damon's goat, Wolf barking all the while?

And when I shouted,"Where's he off to? Call,

Tityrus, your flock,"—you skulked behind the sedge.

DAMŒTAS

Beaten in singing, should he have withheld

The goat my pipe had by its music earned?

That goat was mine, you mayn't p'r'aps know: and he

Owned it himself; but said he could not pay.

MENALCAS

He beat by you? You own a decent pipe?

Used you not, dunce, to stand at the crossroads,

Stifling some lean tune in a squeaky straw?

DAMŒTAS

Shall we then try in turn what each can do?

I stake yon cow—nay hang not back—she comes

23

Twice daily to the pail, is suckling twins.

Say what you'll lay.

MENALCAS

                        I durst not wager aught

Against you from the flock: for I have at home

A father, I have a tyrant stepmother.

Both count the flock twice daily, one the kids.

But what you'll own far handsomer, I'll stake

(Since you will be so mad) two beechen cups,

The carved work of the great Alcimedon.

O'er them the chiseller's skill has traced a vine

That drapes with ivy pale her wide-flung curls.

Two figures in the centre: Conon one,

And—what's that other's name, who'd take a wand

And show the nations how the year goes round;

When you should reap, when stoop behind the plough?

Ne'er yet my lips came near them, safe hid up.

DAMŒTAS

> *For me two cups the selfsame workman made,*
>
> *And clasped with lissom briar the handles round.*
>
> *Orpheus i' the centre, with the woods behind.*
>
> *Ne'er yet my lips came near them, safe hid up.*
>
> *—This talk of cups, if on my cow you've fixed*
>
> *Your eye, is idle.*

MENALCAS

> *Nay you'll not this day*
>
> *Escape me. Name your spot, and I'll be there.*
>
> *Our umpire be—Palæmon; here he comes!*
>
> *I'll teach you how to challenge folks to sing.*

DAMŒTAS

> *Come on, if aught is in you. I'm not loth,*
>
> *I shrink from no man. Only, neighbour, thou*

25

('Tis no small matter) lay this well to heart.

PALÆMON

Say on, since now we sit on softest grass;

And now buds every field and every tree,

And woods are green, and passing fair the year.

Damœtas, lead. Menalcas, follow next.

Sing verse for verse: such songs the Muses love.

DAMŒTAS

With Jove we open. Jove fills everything,

He walks the earth, he listens when I sing.

MENALCAS

Me Phœbus loves. I still have offerings meet

For Phœbus; bay, and hyacinth blushing sweet.

DAMŒTAS

Me Galatea pelts with fruit, and flies

(Wild girl) to the woods: but first would catch my eyes.

MENALCAS

Unbid Amyntas comes to me, my flame;

With Delia's self my dogs are not more tame.

DAMŒTAS

Gifts have I for my fair: who marked but I

The place where doves had built their nest sky-high?

MENALCAS

I've sent my poor gift, which the wild wood bore,

Ten golden apples. Soon I'll send ten more.

DAMŒTAS

Oft Galatea tells me—what sweet tales!

Waft to the god's ears just a part, ye gales!

MENALCAS

At heart Amyntas loves me. Yet what then?

He mates with hunters, I with servingmen.

29

DAMŒTAS

Send me thy Phyllis, good Iolas, now.

To-day's my birthday. When I slay my cow

To help my harvest—come, and welcome, thou.

MENALCAS

Phyllis is my love. When we part, she'll cry;

And fain would bid Iolas' self good-bye.

DAMŒTAS

Wolves kill the flocks, and storms the ripened corn;

And winds the tree; and me a maiden's scorn.

MENALCAS

Rain is the land's delight, weaned kids' the vine;

Big ewes' lithe willow; and one fair face mine.

DAMŒTAS

Pollio loves well this homely muse of mine.

For a new votary fat a calf, ye Nine.

MENALCAS

Pollio makes *songs*. For him a bull demand,

*W*ho butts, whose hoofs already spurn the sand.

DAMŒTAS

*W*ho loves thee, Pollio, go where thou art gone.

For him flow honey, thorns sprout cinnamon.

MENALCAS

*W*ho loathes not Bavius, let him love thy notes,

Mævius:—and yoke the fox, and milk he-goats.

DAMŒTAS

Flowers and ground-strawberries while your prize ye make,

Cold in the grass—fly hence, lads—lurks the snake.

MENALCAS

Sheep, banks are treacherous: draw not over-nigh:

See, now the lordly ram his fleece doth dry.

DAMŒTAS

> *Tityrus, yon she-goats from the river bring.*
>
> *I in due time will wash them at the spring.*

MENALCAS

> *Call, lads, your sheep. Once more our hands, should heat*
>
> *O'ertake the milk, will press in vain the teat.*

DAMŒTAS

> *How rich these vetches, yet how lean my ox.*
>
> *Love kills alike the herdsman and the flocks.*

MENALCAS

> *My lambs—and here love's not in fault, you'll own—*
>
> *Witched by some jealous eye, are skin and bone.*

DAMŒTAS

> *Say in what land—and great Apollo be*
>
> *To me—heaven's arch extends just cubits three.*

MENALCAS

Say in what lands with kings' names grav'n are grown

Flowers—and be Phyllis yours and yours alone.

PALÆMON

Not mine such strife to settle. You have earned

A cow, and you: and whoso else shall e'er

Shrink from love's sweets or prove his bitterness.

Close, lads, the springs. The meads have drunk enough.

E C L O G U E

IV

~~~~~~

Muses of Sicily, a loftier song

Wake we! Some tire of shrubs and myrtles low.

Are woods our theme? Then princely be the woods.

Come are those last days that the Sybil sang:

The ages' mighty march begins anew.

Now comes the virgin, Saturn reigns again:

Now from high heaven descends a wondrous race.

Thou on the newborn babe—who first shall end

36

That age of iron, bid a golden dawn

Upon the broad world—chaste Lucina, smile:

Now thy Apollo reigns. And, Pollio, thou

Shalt be our Prince, when he that grander age

Opens, and onward roll the mighty moons:

Thou, trampling out what prints our crimes have left,

Shalt free the nations from perpetual fear.

While he to bliss shall waken; with the Blest

See the Brave mingling, and be seen of them,

Ruling that world o'er which his father's arm shed peace.—

On thee, child, everywhere shall earth, untilled,

Show'r, her first baby-offerings, vagrant stems

Of ivy, foxglove, and gay briar, and bean;

Unbid the goats shall come big-uddered home,

Nor monstrous lions scare the herded kine.

Thy cradle shall be full of pretty flowers:

Die must the serpent, treacherous poison-plants

Must die; and Syria's roses spring like weeds.

But, soon as thou canst read of hero-deeds

Such as thy father wrought, and understand

What is true worth: the champaign day by day

Shall grow more yellow with the waving corn;

From the wild bramble purpling then shall hang

The grape; and stubborn oaks drop honeydew.

Yet traces of that guile of elder days

Shall linger; bidding men tempt seas in ships,

Gird towns with walls, cleave furrows in the land.

Then a new Tiphys shall arise, to man

New argosies with heroes: then shall be

New wars; and once more shall be bound for Troy,

A mightier Achilles.

      After this,

When thou hast grown and strengthened into man,

The pilot's self shall range the seas no more;

Nor, each land teeming with the wealth of all,

The floating pines exchange their merchandise.

Vines shall not need the pruning-hook, nor earth

The harrow: ploughmen shall unyoke their steers.

Nor then need wool be taught to counterfeit

This hue and that. At will the meadow ram

Shall change to saffron, or the gorgeous tints

Of Tyre, his fair fleece; and the grazing lamb

At will put crimson on.

      So grand an age

Did those three Sisters bid their spindles spin;

Three, telling with one voice the changeless will of Fate.

Oh draw—the time is all but present—near

To thy great glory, cherished child of heaven,

Jove's mighty progeny! And lo! the world,

The round and ponderous world, bows down to thee;

The earth, the ocean-tracts, the depths of heaven.

Lo! nature revels in the coming age.

Oh! may the evening of my days last on,

May breath be mine, till I have told thy deeds!

Not Orpheus then, not Linus, shall outsing

Me: though each vaunts his mother or his sire,

Calliopea this, Apollo that.

Let Pan strive with me, Arcady his judge;

Pan, Arcady his judge, shall yield the palm.

Learn, tiny babe, to read a mother's smile:

Already ten long months have wearied her.

Learn, tiny babe. Him, who ne'er knew such smiles,

Nor god nor goddess bids to board or bed.

E C L O G U E

V

wwwwwwwwwwwwwwwwwwwwwwwwwwwwwwwwwwwwwwwwwwwwwwwwwwwwwwwwwwwwwwwwwwwwwwwwwwww

MENALCAS   MOPSUS

MENALCAS

> *Mopsus, suppose, now two good men have met—*
>
> *You at flute-blowing, as at verses I—*
>
> *We sit down here, where elm and hazel mix.*

MOPSUS

> *Menalcas, meet it is that I obey*
>
> *Mine elder. Lead, or into shade—that shifts*
>
> *At the wind's fancy—or (mayhap the best)*

Into some cave. See here's a cave, o'er which

A wild vine flings her flimsy foliage.

MENALCAS

On these hills one—Amyntas—vies with you.

MOPSUS

Suppose he thought to outsing Phœbus' self?

MENALCAS

Mopsus, begin. If aught you know of flames

That Phyllis kindles; aught of Alcon's worth,

Or Codrus's ill-temper; then begin:

Tityrus meanwhile will watch the grazing kids.

MOPSUS

Aye, I will sing the song which t'other day

On a green beech's bark I cut; and scored

The music, as I wrote. Hear that, and bid

Amyntas vie with me.

MENALCAS

> *As willow lithe*
>
> *Yields to pale olive; as to crimson beds*
>
> *Of roses yields the lowly lavender;*
>
> *So, to my mind, Amyntas yields to you.*

MOPSUS

> *But, lad, no more: we are within the cave.*
>
> (Sings.) *The Nymphs wept Daphnis, slain by ruthless death.*
>
> *Ye, streams and hazels, were their witnesses:*
>
> *When, clasping tight her son's unhappy corpse,*
>
> *"Ruthless," the mother cried, "are gods and stars."*
>
> *None to the cool brooks led in all those days,*
>
> *Daphnis, his fed flocks: no four-footed thing*
>
> *Stooped to the pool, or cropped the meadow grass.*
>
> *How lions of the desert mourned thy death,*
>
> *Forests and mountains wild proclaim aloud.*

'Twas Daphnis taught mankind to yoke in cars

The tiger; lead the winegod's revel on,

And round the tough spear twine the bending leaf.

Vines are the green wood's glory, grapes the vine's:

The bull the cattle's, and the rich land's corn:

Thou art thy people's. When thou metst thy doom,

Both Pales and Apollo left our fields.

In furrows where we dropped big barley seeds,

Spring now rank darnel and the barren reed:

Not violet soft and shining daffodil,

But thistles rear themselves and sharp-spiked thorn.

Shepherds, strow earth with leaves, and hang the springs

With darkness! Daphnis asks of you such rites;

And raise a tomb, and place this rhyme thereon:

"Famed in the green woods, famed beyond the skies,

A fair flock's fairer lord, here Daphnis lies."

MENALCAS

Welcome thy song to me, oh sacred bard,

As, to the weary, sleep upon the grass:

As, in the summer-heat, a bubbling spring

Of sweetest water, that shall slake our thirst.

In song, as on the pipe, thy master's match,

Thou, gifted lad, shalt now our master be.

Yet will I sing in turn, in my poor way,

My song, and raise thy Daphnis to the stars—

Raise Daphnis to the stars. He loved me too.

MOPSUS

Could aught in my eyes such a boon outweigh?

Song-worthy was thy theme: and Stimichon

Told me long since of that same lay of thine.

MENALCAS

(Sings.) *Heaven's unfamiliar floor, and clouds and stars,*

Fair Daphnis, wondering, sees beneath his feet.

Therefore gay revelries fill wood and field,

Pan, and the shepherds, and the Dryad maids.

Wolves plot not harm to sheep, nor nets to deer;

Because kind Daphnis makes it holiday.

The unshorn mountains fling their jubilant voice

Up to the stars: the crags and copses shout

Aloud, "A god, Menalcas, lo! a god."

Oh! be thou kind and good unto thine own!

Behold four altars, Daphnis: two for thee,

Two, piled for Phœbus. Thereupon I'll place

Two cups, with new milk foaming, year by year;

Two goblets filled with richest olive-oil:

And, first with much wine making glad the feast—

At the fireside in snowtime, 'neath the trees

In harvest—pour, rare nectar, from the can

The wines of Chios. Lyctian Ægon then

Shall sing me songs, and to Damœtas' pipe

Alphesibœus dance his Satyr-dance.

And this shalt thou lack never: when we pay

The Nymphs our vows, and when we cleanse the fields.

While boars haunt mountain-heights, and fishes streams,

Bees feed on thyme, and grasshoppers on dew,

Thy name, thy needs, thy glory shall abide.

As Bacchus and as Ceres, so shalt thou

Year after year the shepherd's vows receive;

So bind him to the letter of his vow.

MOPSUS

What can I give thee, what, for such a song?

Less sweet to me the coming South-wind's sigh,

The sea-wave breaking on the shore, the noise

Of rivers, rushing through the stony vales.

MENALCAS

First I shall offer you this brittle pipe.

This taught me how to sing, "For one fair face";

This taught me "Whose flock? Melibœus's?"

MOPSUS

Take thou this crook; which oft Antigenes

Asked—and he then was loveable—in vain;

Brass-tipped and even-knotted—beautiful!

E C L O G U E

VI

~~~~~~

My *muse first stooped to trifle, like the Greek's,*

In numbers; and, unblushing, dwelt in woods.

I sang embattled kings: but Cynthius plucked

My ear, and warned me: "Tityrus, fat should be

A shepherd's wethers, but his lays thin-drawn."

So—for enough and more will strive to tell,

Varus, thy deeds, and pile up grisly wars—

53

On pipe of straw will I my wood-notes sing:

I sing not all unbid. Yet oh! should one

Smit by great love, should one read this my lay—

Then with thee, Varus, shall our myrtle-groves,

And all these copses, ring. Right dearly loves

Phœbus the page that opens with thy name.

On, sisters!

> *—Chromis and Mnasylus saw*

(Two lads) Silenus in a cave asleep:

As usual, swoln with yesterday's debauch.

Just where it fell his garland lay hard by;

And on worn handle hung his ponderous can.

They—for the old man oft had cheated each

Of promised songs—draw near, and make his wreaths

Fetters to bind him. Ægle makes a third

(Ægle, the loveliest of the Naiad maids)

To back their fears: and, as his eyes unclose,

Paints brow and temples red with mulberry.

He, laughing at the trick, cries, "Wherefore weave

These fetters? Lads, unbind me: 'tis enough

But to have seemed to have me in your power.

Ye ask a song; then listen. You I'll pay

With song: for her I've other meed in store."

And forthwith he begins. Then might you see

Move to the music Faun and forest-beast,

And tall oaks bow their heads. Not so delights

Parnassus in Apollo: not so charmed

At Orpheus Rhodope and Ismarus.

For this he sang: How, drawn from that vast void,

Gathered the germs of earth and air and sea

And liquid flame. How the Beginning sprang

Thence, and the young world waxed into a ball.

Then Earth, grown harder, walled the sea-god off

In seas, and slowly took substantial form:

Till on an awed world dawned the wondrous sun,

And straight from heaven, by clouds unbroken, fell

The showers: as woods first bourgeoned, here and there

A wild beast wandering over hills unknown.

Of Pyrrha casting stones, and Saturn's reign,

The stolen fire, the eagles of the rock,

He sings: and then, beside what spring last seen,

The sailors called for Hylas—till the shore

All rang with "Hylas," "Hylas":—and consoles

(Happy if horned herds never had been born)

With some fair bullock's love Pasiphae.

Ah! hapless maid! What madness this of thine?

Once a king's daughters made believe to low,

And ranged the leas: but neither stooped to ask

Those base beasts' love: though each had often feared

To find the ploughman's gear about her neck,

And felt on her smooth brow for budding horns.

Ah! hapless maid! Thou roam'st from hill to hill:

He under some dark oak—his snowy side

Cushioned on hyacinths—chews the pale-green grass,

Or woos some favourite from the herd. "Close, Nymphs,

Dictæan Nymphs, oh close the forest-glades!

If a bull's random footprints by some chance

Should greet me! Lured, may be, by greener grass,

Or in the herd's wake following, vagrant kine

May bring him straight into my father's fold!"

—Then sings he of that maid who paused to gaze

At the charmed apples—and surrounds with moss,

Bitter tree-moss, the daughters of the Sun,

Till up they spring tall alders.—Then he sings

How Gallus, wandering to Parnassus' stream,

A sister led to the Aonian hills,

And, in a mortal's honour, straight uprose

The choir of Phœbus: How that priest of song,

The shepherd Linus,—all his hair with flowers

And bitter parsley shining,—spake to him.

"Take—lo! the Muses give it thee—this pipe.

Once that Ascræan's old: to this would he

Sing till the sturdy mountain-ash came down.

Sing thou on this, whence sprang Æolia's grove,

Till in no wood Apollo glory more."

So on and on he sang: How Nisus, famed

In story, troubled the Dulichian ships;

And in the deep seas bid her sea-dogs rend

The trembling sailors. Tereus' tale he told,

How he was changed: what banquet Philomel,

What present, decked for him: and how she flew

To the far wilderness; and flying paused—

(Poor thing)—to flutter round her ancient home.

All songs which one day Phœbus sang to charmed

Eurotas—and the laurels learnt them off—

He sang. The thrilled vales fling them to the stars

Till Hesper bade them house and count their flocks,

And journeyed all unwelcome up the sky.

E C L O G U E

VII

<hr>

MELIBŒUS   **CORYDON**   **THYRSIS**

MELIBŒUS

Daphnis was seated 'neath a murmurous oak,

When Corydon and Thyrsis (so it chanced)

Had driv'n their two flocks—one of sheep, and one

Of teeming goats—together: herdsmen both,

Both in life's spring, and able well to sing,

Or, challenged, to reply. To that same spot

I, guarding my young myrtles from the frost,

Find my goat strayed, the patriarch of the herd:

And straight spy Daphnis. He, espying me

In turn, cries, "Melibœus! hither, quick!

Thy goat, and kids, are safe. And if thou hast

An hour to spare, sit down beneath the shade.

Hither unbid will troop across the leas

The kine to drink: green Mincius fringes here

His banks with delicate bullrush, and a noise

Of wild bees rises from the sacred oak."

What could I do? Alcippe I had none,

Nor Phyllis, to shut up my new-weaned lambs:

Then, there was war on foot—a mighty war—

Thyrsis and Corydon!—So in the end

I made my business wait upon their sport.—

64

So singing verse for verse—that well the Muse

Might mark it—they began their singing match.

Thus Corydon, thus Thyrsis sang in turn.

(They sing.)

CORYDON

"Ye Fountain Nymphs, my loves! Grant me to sing

Like Codrus—next Apollo's rank his lines—

Or here—if all may scarce do everything—

I'll hang my pipe up on these sacred pines."

THYRSIS

"Swains! a new minstrel deck with ivy now,

Till Codrus burst with envy! Or, should he

Flatter o'ermuch, twine foxglove o'er my brow,

Lest his knave's-flattery spoil the bard to be."

CORYDON

""To Dian, from young Micon: this boar's head,

65

And these broad antlers of a veteran buck.'

Full-length in marble—ankle-bound with red

Buskins—I'll rear her, should to-day bring luck."

THYRSIS

"Ask but this bowl, Priapus, and this cake

Each year: for poor the garden thou dost keep.

Our small means made thee marble: whom we'll make

Of gold, should lambing multiply our sheep."

CORYDON

"Maid of the seas! more sweet than Hybla's thyme,

Graceful as ivy, white as is the swan!

When home the fed flocks wend at evening's prime,

Then come—if aught thou car'st for Corydon."

THYRSIS

"Hark! bitterer than wormwood may I be,

Bristling as broom, as drifted sea-weed cheap,

If this day seem not a long year to me!

Home, home for very shame, my o'er-fed sheep!"

CORYDON

"Ye mossy rills, and lawns more soft than dreams,

Thinly roofed over by these leaves of green:

From the great heat—now summer's come, now teems

The jocund vine with buds—my cattle screen."

THYRSIS

"Warm hearth, good faggots, and great fires you'll find

In my home: black with smoke are all its planks:

We laugh, who're in it, at the chill north wind,

As wolves at troops of sheep, mad streams at banks."

CORYDON

"*Here furry chestnuts rise and juniper:*

Heaped 'neath each tree the fallen apples lie:

All smiles. But, once let fair Alexis stir

From off these hills—and lo! the streams are dry."

THYRSIS

"*Thirsts in parched lands and dies the blighted grass;*

Vines lend no shadow to the mountain height;

But groves shall bloom again, when comes my lass;

And in glad showers Jove descend in might."

CORYDON

"*Poplars Alcides likes, and Bacchus vines;*

Fair Venus myrtle, and Apollo bay;

But while to hazel-leaves my love inclines,

Nor bays nor myrtles greater are than they."

THYRSIS

"*Fair in woods ash; and pine on garden-grass:*

On tall cliffs fir; by pools the poplar-tree.

But if thou come here oft, sweet Lycidas,

Lawn-pine and mountain-ash must yield to thee."

MELIBŒUS

All this I've heard before: remember well

How Thyrsis strove in vain against defeat.

From that day forth 'twas 'Corydon' for me.

E C L O G U E

VIII

~~~~~~

DAMON   ALPHESIBŒUS

Alphesibœus's and Damon's muse—

Charmed by whose strife the steer forgot to graze;

Whose notes made lynxes motionless, and bade

Rivers turn back and listen—sing we next:

Alphesibœus's and Damon's muse.

Winn'st thou the crags of great Timavus now,

71

Or skirtest strands where break Illyrian seas?

I know not. But oh when shall that day dawn

When I may tell thy deeds? give earth thy lays,

That match alone the pomp of Sophocles?

With thee began, with thee shall end, my song:

Accept what thou didst ask; and round thy brow

Twine this poor ivy with thy victor bays.

'Twas at the hour when night's cold shadow scarce

Had left the skies; when, blest by herdsmen, hangs

The dewdrop on the grass; that Damon leaned

On his smooth olive-staff, and thus began:

DAMON

"Wake, morning star! Prevent warm day, and come!

While, duped and humbled, I—because I loved

Nisa with all a husband's love—complain;

And call the gods (though naught their cognizance

Availed) at my last hour, a dying man.

Begin, my flute, a song of Arcady.

"There forests murmur aye, and pines discourse;

And lovelorn swains, and Pan, who first reclaimed

From idleness the reed, hath audience there,

Begin, my flute, a song of Arcady.

"Nisa—is aught impossible in love?—

Is given to Mopsus. Griffins next will mate

With mares: our children see the coward deer

Come with the hound to drink. Go, shape the torch,

Mopsus! fling, bridegroom, nuts! Thou lead'st a wife

Home, and o'er Œta peers the evening star.

Begin, my flute, a song of Arcady.

74

"*Oh, mated with a worthy husband! thou*

Who scorn'st mankind—abhorr'st this pipe, these goats

Of mine, and shaggy brows, and hanging beard:

Nor think'st that gods can see what mortals do!

    Begin, my flute, a song of Arcady.

"*Within our orchard-walls I saw thee first,*

A wee child with her mother—(I was sent

To guide you)—gathering apples wet with dew.

Ten years and one I scarce had numbered then;

Could scarce on tiptoe reach the brittle boughs.

I saw, I fell, I was myself no more.

    Begin, my flute, a song of Arcady.

"*Now know I what love is. On hard rocks born*

Tmaros, or Rhodope, or they who dwell

In utmost Africa do father him;

No child of mortal blood or lineage.

Begin, my flute, a song of Arcady.

"In her son's blood a mother dipped her hands

At fierce love's bidding. Hard was her heart too—

Which harder? her heart or that knavish boy's?

Knavish the boy, and hard was her heart too.

    Begin, my flute, a song of Arcady.

"Now let the wolf first turn and fly the sheep:

Hard oaks bear golden apples: daffodil

Bloom on the alder: and from myrtle-stems

Ooze richest amber. Let owls vie with swans;

And be as Orpheus—Orpheus in the woods,

Arion with the dolphins—every swain.

    (Begin, my flute, a song of Arcady.)

"And earth become mid-ocean. Woods, farewell!

Down from some breezy mountain height to the waves

I'll fling me. Take this last gift ere I die.

    Unlearn, my flute, the songs of Arcady."

77

Thus Damon. How the other made reply,

Sing, sisters. Scarce may all do everything.

ALPHESIBŒUS

"Fetch water: wreathe yon altar with soft wool:

And burn rich vervain and brave frankincense;

That I may try my lord's clear sense to warp

With dark rites. Naught is lacking save the songs.

    Bring, songs, bring Daphnis from the city home.

"Songs can bring down the very moon from heaven.

Circe with songs transformed Ulysses' crew.

Songs shall in sunder burst the cold grass snake.

    Bring, songs, bring Daphnis from the city home.

"Three threads about thee, of three several hues,

I twine; and thrice—(odd numbers please the god)—

Carry thy image round the altar-stones.

 Bring, songs, bring Daphnis from the city home.

"Weave, Amaryllis, in three knots three hues.

Just weave and say: 'I'm weaving chains of love.'

 Bring, songs, bring Daphnis from the city home.

"As this clay hardens, melts this wax, at one

And the same flame: so Daphnis 'neath my love.

Strew meal, and light with pitch the crackling bay.

Daphnis burns me; for Daphnis burn these bays.

 Bring, songs, bring Daphnis from the city home.

"Be his such longing as the heifer feels,

When, faint with seeking her lost mate through copse

And deepest grove, beside some water-brook

In the green grass she sinks in her despair,

Nor cares to yield possession to the night.

Be his such longing: mine no wish to heal.

 Bring, songs, bring Daphnis from the city home.

"Pledges of love, these clothes the traitor once

Bequeathed me. I commit them, Earth, to thee

Here at my threshold. He is bound by these.

 Bring, songs, bring Daphnis from the city home.

"These deadly plants great Mœris gave to me,

In Pontus plucked: in Pontus thousands grow.

By their aid have I seen him skulk in woods

A wolf, unsepulchre the buried dead,

And charm to other fields the standing corn.

 Bring, songs, bring Daphnis from the city home.

80

"Go, Amaryllis, ashes in thy hand:

Throw them—and look not backwards—o'er thy head

Into a running stream. These next I'll try

On Daphnis; who regards not gods nor songs.

Bring, songs, bring Daphnis from the city home.

"See! While I hesitate, a quivering flame

Hath clutched the wood, self-issuing from the ash.

May this mean good! Something—for Hylas too

Barks at the gate—it must mean. Is it true?

Or are we lovers dupes of our own dreams?

Cease, songs, cease. Daphnis comes from the city home!"

E C L O G U E

IX

〜〜〜〜〜〜〜〜〜〜〜〜〜〜〜〜〜〜〜〜〜〜〜〜〜〜〜〜〜〜〜〜〜〜〜〜〜

LYCIDAS   MŒRIS

LYCIDAS

Mœris, on foot? and on the road to town?

MŒRIS

Oh Lycidas!—we live to tell—how one—

(Who dreamed of this?)—a stranger—holds our farm,

And says,"'Tis mine: its ancient lords, begone!"

Beaten, cast down—for Chance is lord of all—

82

We send him—bootlessly mayhap—these kids.

LYCIDAS

Yet all, I heard, from where we lose yon hills,

With gradual bend down-sloping to the brook,

And those old beeches, broken columns now,

Had your Menalcas rescued by his songs.

MŒRIS

Thou heardst. Fame said so. But our songs avail,

Mœris, no more 'mid warspears than, they say,

Dodona's doves may, when the eagle stoops.

A boding raven from a rifted oak

Warned me, by this means or by that to nip

This strange strife in the bud: or dead were now

Thy Mœris; dead were great Menalcas too.

LYCIDAS

Could such curse fall on man? Had we so near

Lost thee, Menalcas, and thy pleasantries?

Who then would sing the nymphs? Who strow with flowers

The ground, or train green darkness o'er the springs?

And oh! that song, which I (saying ne'er a word)

Copied one day—(while thou wert off to see

My darling, Amaryllis)—from thy notes:

"Feed, while I journey but a few short steps,

Tityrus, my goats: and, Tityrus, when they've fed,

Lead them to drink: and cross not by the way

The he-goat's path: his horns are dangerous."

MŒRIS

But that to Varus, that unfinished one!

"Varus! thy name, if Mantua still be ours—

(Mantua! to poor Cremona all too near)—

Shall tuneful swans exalt unto the stars."

LYCIDAS

> *Begin, if in thee's aught. So may not yews*
>
> *Of Cyrnus lure thy bees: so, clover-fed,*
>
> *Thy cattle teem with milk. Me too the muse*
>
> *Hath made a minstrel: I have songs; and me*
>
> *The swains call "poet." But I heed them not.*
>
> *For scarce yet sing I as the great ones sing,*
>
> *But, a goose, cackle among piping swans.*

MŒRIS

> *Indeed, I am busy turning o'er and o'er—*
>
> *In hopes to recollect it—in my brain*
>
> *A song, and not a mean one, Lycidas.*

> *"Come, Galatea! sport'st thou in the waves?*
>
> *Here spring is purpling; thick by river-banks*
>
> *Bloom the gay flowers; white poplar climbs above*

The caves, and young vines plait a roof between.

Come! and let mad seas beat against the shore."

LYCIDAS

What were those lines that once I heard thee sing,

All uncompanioned on a summer night—

I know the music, if I had the words.

MŒRIS

"Daphnis! why watch those old-world planets rise?

Lo! onward marches sacred Cæsar's star,

The star that made the valleys laugh with corn,

And grapes grow ruddier upon sunny hills.

Sow, Daphnis, pears, whereof thy sons shall eat."

—Time carries all—our memories e'en—away.

Well I remember how my boyish songs

Would oft outlast the livelong summer day.

87

And now they're all forgot. His very voice

Hath Mœris lost: on Mœris wolves have looked.

—But oft thou'lt hear them from Menalcas yet.

LYCIDAS

Thy pleas but draw my passion out. And lo!

All hushed to listen is the wide sea-floor,

And laid the murmurings of the soughing winds.

And now we're half-way there. I can descry

Bianor's grave. Here, Mœris, where the swains

Are raking off the thick leaves, let us sing.

Or, if we fear lest night meanwhile bring up

The rain clouds, singing let us journey on—

(The way will seem less tedious)—journey on

Singing: and I will ease thee of thy load.

MŒRIS

Cease, lad. We'll do what lies before us now:

Then sing our best, when comes the Master home.

E C L O G U E

X

~~~~~~

GALLUS

Oh Arethuse, let this last task be mine!

One song—a song Lycoris' self may read—

My Gallus asks: who'd grudge one song to him?

So, when thou slid'st beneath Sicilian seas,

May ne'er salt Doris mix her stream with thine:

Begin: and sing—while yon blunt muzzles search

90

The underwood—of Gallus torn by love.

We lack not audience: woods take up the notes.

Where were ye, Naiad Nymphs, in grove or glen,

When Gallus died of unrequited love?

Not heights of Pindus or Parnassus, no

Aonian Aganippe kept ye then.

Him e'en the laurels wept and myrtle-groves.

Stretched 'neath the lone cliff, piny Mænalus

And chill Lycæum's stones all wept for him.

The sheep stood round. They think not scorn of us;

And think not scorn, O priest of song, of them.

Sheep fair Adonis fed beside the brooks.

The shepherds came. The lazy herdsmen came.

Came, from the winter acorns dripping-wet,

Menalcas. "Whence," all ask, "this love of thine?"

Apollo came: and, "Art thou mad," he saith,

"Gallus? Thy love, through bristling camps and snows,

Tracks now another's steps." Silvanus came,

Crowned with his woodland glories: to and fro

Rocked the great lilies and the fennel bloom.

Pan came, Arcadia's Pan (I have seen him, red

With elder-berries and with cinnabar):

"Is there no end?" quoth he: "Love heeds not this:

Tears sate not cruel Love: nor rills the leas,

Nor the bees clover, nor green boughs the goat."

But he rejoins sad-faced: "Yet sing this song

Upon your hills, Arcadians! none but ye

Can sing. Oh! pleasantly will rest my bones,

If pipe of yours shall one day tell my loves.

Oh! had I been as you are! kept your flocks,

Or gleaned, a vintager, your mellow grapes!

A Phyllis, an Amyntas—whom you will—

Had been my passion—what if he be dark?

Violets are dark and hyacinths are dark.—

And now should we be sitting side by side,

Willows around us and a vine o'erhead,

He carolling, or plucking garlands she.

—Here are cold springs, Lycoris, and soft lawns,

And woods: with thee I'd here decay and die.

Now, for grim war accoutred, all for love,

In the fray's centre I await the foe:

Thou, in a far land—out the very thought!—

Gazest (ah wilful!) upon Alpine snows

And the froz'n Rhine—without me—all alone!

May that frost harm not thee! that jagged ice

Cut ne'er thy dainty feet! I'll go, and play

My stores of music—fashioned for the lyre

Of Chalcis—on the pipe of Arcady.

My choice is made. In woods, mid wild beasts' dens,

I'll bear my love, and carve it on the trees:

That with their growth, my loves may grow and grow.

Banded with nymphs I'll roam o'er Mænalus,

Or hunt swift boars; and circle with my dogs,

Unrecking of the cold, Parthenia's glades.

Already over crag and ringing grove

I am borne in fancy: laugh as I let loose

The Cretan arrow from the Parthian bow:

Pooh! will this heal thy madness? will that god

Learn mercy from the agonies of men?

'Tis past: again nymphs, music, fail to please.

Again I bid the very woods begone.

No deed of mine can change him: tho' I drink

Hebrus in mid December: tho' I plunge

In snows of Thrace, the dripping winter's snows:

Tho', when the parched bark dies on the tall elm,

'Neath Cancer's star I tend the Æthiop's sheep.

Love's lord of all. Let me too yield to Love."

*   *   *

—Sung are, oh holy ones, your minstrel's songs:

Who sits here framing pipes with slender reed.

In Gallus' eyes will ye enhance their worth:

Gallus—for whom each hour my passion grows,

As swell green alders when the spring is young.

I rise. The shadows are the singer's bane:

Baneful the shadow of the juniper.

E'en the flocks like not shadow. Go—the star

Of morning breaks—go home, my full-fed sheep.

96